EPHES

AND
THE HOUSE OF VIRGIN MARY

İ.Akan ATİLA
ARCHAEOLOGIST

Özcan ATALAY
ACETATE ILLUSTRATION

NECMİ ÇETİN
Güney
BOOKS

CONTENTS

© PUBLICATION & DISTRIBUTOR
Güney Kartpostal Ve Turistik Yayıncılık
CENTRE: KIŞLA MAH. 47. SOKAK. KÖKEN APT. 5/3 ANTALYA
📞 (0242) 242 99 23   📠 (0242) 241 97 97
BRANCH: ATATÜRK MAH. 1069 SOK. 10/A SELÇUK / İZMİR
📞 (0232) 892 72 48
📧 INFO@GUNEYKARTPOSTAL.COM   WWW.GUNEYKARTPOSTAL.COM
ISBN 978-975-699-448-1

TEXT: İ.Akan ATİLA Archaeologist
ACETATE ILLUSTRATION: Özcan ATALAY
GRAPHIC DESIGN: Korhan KARASU
PHOTOS: Gani BAKIR - İ. Akan ATİLA - Necmi ÇETİN
Ceylan ÇETİNTÜRK - Ali Rıza ÇELEBİ
TRANSLATION: Adnan ŞENTÜRK
PRINTING: OLUŞUR BASIM A.Ş

12. EDITION 2016

3

THE PLAN OF EPHESUS

1-THE TOMB OF THE EVANGELIST LUKE
2-THE UPPER GYMNASIUM BATHS
3-THE STOA BASILEIOS (THE ROYAL WALK)
4-THE ODEION
5-THE CITY HALL (PRYTANEION)
6-THE GOVERNMENT AGORA
7-THE MONUMENT OF MEMMIUS
8-THE BUILDING OF POLLIO AND THE FOUNTAIN OF DOMITIANUS

9-THE FOUNTAIN OF LAECANIUS BASSUS (HYDREKDOKHEION)
10-THE TEMPLE OF DOMITIANUS
11-THE GATE OF HERCULES
12-KURETES STREET
13-THE FOUNTAIN OF TRAIANUS
14-THE BATHS OF VARIUS (SCOLASTIKIA)
15-THE TEMPLE OF HADRIANUS
16-HOUSES ON THE SLOPES

17-THE LATRINA (PUBLIC LAVATORY)
18-THE OCTAGON AND THE FOUNTAIN OF THE CITY-FOUNDER ANDROKLOS
19-THE LOVE HOUSE
20-THE LIBRARY OF CELSUS
21-THE GATES OF MAZAEUS AND MITHRIDATES
22-THE TETRAGONOS AGORA
23-THE STOA OF NERO
24-THE MARBLE STREET

25-THE GRAND THEATRE
26-THE HELLENISTIC FOUNTAIN
27-THE ARKADIANE (HARBOR STREET)
28-THE THEATRE GYMNASIUM
29-THE CHURCH OF MARY

30-THE HARBOR BATHS
31-THE TEMPLE OF SERAPEION
32-THE CAVE OF ST. PAUL
33-THE STADION
34-THE CAVE OF THE SEVEN SLEEPERS

35-THE ARTEMISION (THE TEMPLE OF ARTEMIS)
36-THE BATHS OF ISA BEY
37-THE MOSQUE OF ISA BEY
38-THE CHURCH OF ST. JOHN
39-THE HOUSE OF THE VIRGIN MARY

THE TOMB OF THE EVANGELIST LUKE

This is located to the south of the road and east of the parking lot by the upper entrance. J. T. Wood observed the bull reliefs carved on the wall support in the east, as well as the sign of the cross, during his first excavation at Ephesus in 1825. He named the structure "The Tomb of Luke the Evangelist" taking into consideration that the fact that the bull is the symbol of Luke the Evangelist. Dating from the 2nd century A.D., the tomb was constructed upon the ruins of an older structure, whose function is today unknown. Within the infrastructure of the Roman podium there are some rooms surrounding the massive central supports and the upper side of the podium is surrounded by columns. During the Early Byzantine period

in the 5th and 6th centuries, this Roman structure was converted into a church and an apse was added and, in recent excavations some traces concerning the Evangelist John were found. The church is accessed via the west and the east stairs and stands upon a Roman period podium without any columns. This central structure on the top is connected to the church through a narrow staircase beneath and the remains of numerous murals indicate that this structure was richly embellished. The southern entrance to the crypt is covered by spolien wall supports on two sides. That on the west side is ornamented with a cross ornament while the east side has a cross and also a bull carved in relief. During excavations several tombs of children were found around this structur

7

THE UPPER GYMNASIUM BATHS

The Great Baths located at the entrance to the ancient city of Ephesus, was in error named the Varius Baths, the excavation of these baths are not yet completed. It was constructed in the hillside of Mount Pion (Panayır Dağı) to the east of the Agora and the four grand chambers of these baths, those on the northern side were built partially into the rock. It differs from the typical plan of Roman baths as it has as asymmetrical plan, although it resembles the other baths of Ephesus in that it has a Frigidarium (Cold Section), an Apodyterium (Dressing Section), a Tepidarium (Warm Section), a Calidarium (Hot Section) and a Sudatorium (Sweating Section). The Baths were heated through the "Hypocaust" system, where hot air was circulated beneath the paved floor. In the west chamber (the Calidarium), there are huge windows with a bathing pool and seven niches facing west. In the south there is a public lavatory (Latrina) and many smaller adjoining rooms where trading was conducted. These baths were ruined many times due to seismic activity but they were repeatedly repaired following seismic damage. On the western and southern sides of the baths are chambers with floors decorated with mosaics and it is understood from an inscription on the mosaic floor that the construction of this phase of the structure was financed by a city chamberlain named Asclepius in the 5th century A.D. Some statues of Aphrodite, Dionysos, Hygeia and Pan were recovered during the excavation of this bath complex and are exhibited today in the İzmir Museum of Archeology.

THE STOA BASILEIOS (THE ROYAL WALK)

THE STOA BASILEIOS (THE ROYAL WALK)

This structure is located to the southwest of the Odeon and north of the Agora. According to the inscription found within the structure it was constructed in the 1st century A.D. by C. Sextilius Pollio and his daughter Ofilia Bassa. The Stoic Basilica was 165 m. long, of two storeys and three naves. There were 67 columns in the Ionic order carrying bull-head capitals, which formed the middle nave and these columns, destroyed by an earthquake only 12 years after its construction, were rebuilt and the rear wall of the structure was reconstructed using marble orthostat blocks and the structure was strengthened by adding additional columns with Corinthian capitals between the inner columns. The west part of the stoa was covered by a Khalkidikum during the reign of Emperor Nero. The platform constructed of rusticated masonry,

where the path from the Prytaneion meets Domitianus Square, extends for 15,90 metres in front of the west terrace wall of the Government Agora. This stoa, which was connected to the middle nave of the Basilica by an arch and which was constructed with half-columns in the Ionic order and wall supports, accords with the additional Basilica structures described by Vitruvius (V 1,4) as being a khalkidikum. The three chambers of this structure are accessed through three gates from the Domitianus Square. Facing the Domitianus Square, on the gates there is a wall architrave upon which some letters forming the inscription have been intentionally removed and replaced

by bronze letters. This inscription with its missing letters is thought to have been connected with Emperor Nero who reigned from 43 to 68 A.D. In Late Antiquity, during the reign of Theodosius, some parts of this stoa were demolished and the whole structure was then converted into a church with an apse added to the western side and this structure was then known as the Bazaar of Theodosius. There is a Khalkidikum ceremonial gate to the east of this structure and this gate was decorated with statues of the Emperor Octavianus Augustus and his wife Livia. These statues are today exhibited in the Museum of Ephesus.

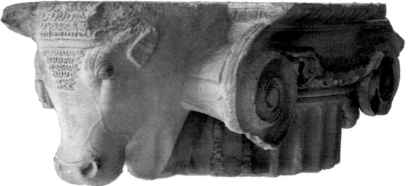

THE ODEION

This is the structure located on the hillside of Mount Pion that was defined as the City Council Hall (Bouleuterion) or Concert Hall (Odeion) after its discovery by J. T. Wood, who excavated at Ephesus in the 19th century. The Odeion was the place where the members of the City Council, comprising the wealthy people of Ephesus and Kuretes (Priests) gathered and

Basilica, on the east and west corners of the stage structure. There are also entrances from the gates in the northern wall and in the high arched spaces on the edges of the parados. There is a broad diazoma (walkway) which divides the seating area into two. foundations. Its seating capacity xareas (cavea) are divided by radial stairs into sections called kerkis. It is presumed from the architectural parts and the traces that were

spectacular stage. In order to protect the audience from the sun and rain, small structures such as the Bouleuterion and Odeion, were covered by a fixed roof. These roofs were usually covered by wood and fired clay tiles, supported by a big triangular sculptures of Emperor Verus, a wooden truss framework. The young Faustina, a torso of Silenos and Mousa Erate were amongst the sculptural finds made by J. T.

discussed the future of the city and also listened to musical concerts. It is understood from the inscriptions on the architrave that it was constructed by P. Vedius Antonius and his wife Flavia Papiana, who were amongst the wealthy inhabitants of the city in the 2nd century A.D. Its seating area (cavea) is encircled with a thick semi-circular wall and is supported by vaulted foundations. Its seating capacity is for approximately 1500 people. Entrance to the diazoma is provided by the gates of the Stoic

found in the excavations that there used to be a gallery adorned with red marble columns behind the upper seating area (cavea). The ground of the orchestra, which is between the lowest seating area and the stage, was originally covered with a stone slab pavement. The front of the stage (scaenae frons) is of two storeys with columns and aediculas (small niches) that were filled with statues and the stage can be entered through five smaller gates. Today there is not much is left of this

Wood in the 19th century, and which were taken to the British Museum, London. The restoration work in the Odeion was conducted by the Seljuk Museum of Ephesus in 1970 and in 1990.

11

THE CITY HALL (PRYTANEION)

This is one of the official buildings constructed during the Augustan Period in the Government Quarter of the city. There is an entrance to the Prytaneion from the North Stoa. There is a place where food and the sacred altar of fire were located, constructed from ashlar masonry in the center of the main residence which has columns carrying heart shaped relief carvings. Adjacent to the north and west side of this grand hall are smaller chambers, whose particular functions are unknown. The list of the names of the Priests (Kuretes) together with religious texts were found, inscribed on the partially raised 6 Doric columns during the restoration work in front of the Prytaneion. One of the duties of the Kuretes was to ensure that the sacred fire was kept alight at all times. This eternal flame was understood to symbolize and ensure the city's continued existence. This hearth in the Prytaneion is proof that Hestia Bulaia, the Goddess of home and the protector of the city, was worshipped in this structure. The other duties of Hestia were to organize the feasts given every year in honor of her twins Artemis and Apollo. On the 6th of May the statue of Artemis was taken from the Temple of Artemis by a procession, among which there were the Kuretes and, according to specific ceremonial rites, the statue was paraded around the city of Ephesus and then taken back to the Temple of Artemis. Attended by thé most important guests of the city and privileged people worthy of this honor, banquets were held related to political - religious events in the grand hall of the Prytaneion and these meetings were financed by the government. In the 2nd century, other gods were added to the cult of Hestia, such as Apollo, the God of Prophecy and Demeter. Amongst the finds from the 1956 excavation of the Prytaneion, in addition to the inscriptions, which are extremely important for religious history, were the finds of three Roman copies of the Artemis Ephesia cult statue, made by Emperor Octavianus in the Augustan Period, which were entombed after the 4th century earthquake for religious reasons, to protect the city from future earthquakes (these statues are today displayed in Chamber 6 of the Seljuk Museum of Ephesus). After the 4th century earthquake, the columns carrying inscriptions and most of the other construction material from this building were reused in reconstruction work on the Kuretes Street (the name given to this street comes from these reused columns) and in the Scolastikia Bath-house.

THE GOVERNMENT AGORA

There is a broad space accessed via a few stairs lying directly to the west of the Stoa Basileios. The construction of this Government Agora, initially founded in the Late Hellenistic Period, was completed in the Late Augustan Period. The east side of this Agora area, which is supported by ashlar stonework from the west, was leveled and the structure was 160 m. long and 58 m. wide, being added to from the west. In ancient times the Agora was the central place in the city where religious and political meetings and debates took place and the important issues of the city were discussed and resolved and from where the city was administered. There are the fountains of Laecanius Bassus Hydrekdocheion and Domitianus located at the end of the South Stoa and in the southwest corner of the Government Agora's terrace wall. The Khalkidikum is situated at the end of the north stoa and in front of the terrace wall adjacent to the Fountain of Domitianus, while the three-naved Stoa Basileios is to the north of the Agora. In the South Stoa, dating from the first period of construction, there are two gates with two naves constructed in the Doric order. In addition, there is an entrance to the Agora from the east corner of the South Stoa and the Doric Gate from the South Street. Today only two Doric order supports from the gate walls are extant. The pediment, which was adorned with aegis reliefs, defined a gate structure with a tall and broad roof, supported by four columns in the Doric order. The columns, barrel vaults and supports remain in their original locations. From its architectural style it is thought this Doric Gate dates from around the 2nd or 1st century B.C. From this gate structure, it is possible to pass into the Doric style two naved South Stoa of the Government Agora. There are today only a limited number of architectural remains from this Stoa. The rear wall is preserved in a good condition and has an extensive marble bench in front of it. Sometraces of another badly preserved Doric Gate, which opens to Domitianus Street from the west corner of the South Stoa, were found in these excavations. Initally there was only one stoa with one nave on the northern side of the Government Agora. In the second phase, contemporary with the Southern stoa, the Northern stoa had a hall with single-nave columns and a small chamber in the western corner. Later many architectural modifications were made to this stoa. The western edge of the north Stoa extended in parallel to the Cortege Path which crossed this area.

THE MONUMENT OF MEMMIUS

In the third quarter of the century B.C. a monument that was constructed north of Domitian Square, at the north corner of Kuretes Street. It is one of the few architectural monuments dating from the Late Hellenistic period that has survived to the present day at Ephesus. In this monument, discovered in 1959/60 an inscription was found on the first level on an architrave which recorded the name Memmius in both Greek and Latin. The monument was erected in honor of C. Memmius, the nephew of the Roman dictator Sulla, gaius Memmius, who was one of the prominent people of the city. Regarding the architectural finds made during these excavations, it

had circular finds facing east, south and west. The arches of the niches were supported by caryatids, which carried capitals in the form of baskets. The fourth side which faces the roadway was probably not decorated. From the architectural finds, this monument, made out of bottom to the upper niches, over an upper Attica layer, decorated by extending half reliefs, in which. From a scene that probably really similar scenes which belonged to this structure, it was understood that this structure had the same as the traditional tower-shaped Hellenistic tombs and monuments. According to the plan there was an upper level facing in three directions, supported by columns. It is thought

that the reliefs were represented in the upper chamber and soldiers on the walls of the upper chamber. The people concerned the prominent people of the Memmius family and the virtues of Memmius were depicted in a personalized manner. It is possible that the other structure, adorned with griffin and bull capitals, and various textile pieces, which are in the proximity to this monument of Memmius, also belonged to this structure.

THE BUILDING OF POLLIO AND THE FOUNTAIN OF DOMITIANUS

The Building of Pollio: This monument, which faces the Domitianus Square, in front of the west terrace wall of the Government Agora, is between the Khalkidikum and the fountain of Domitianus. It was constructed by the foster son of C. Sextilius Pollio, because of his important contributions to the city of Ephesus, in this area which was allotted by the city administration in honor of C. Sextilius Pollio and this monument is also the cenotaph of C. Sextilius Pollio. It is known from the Latin and Greek inscriptions that this structure was constructed in 92-93 A.D. There is a monumental pedestal (partially repaired or reconstructed) covered with marble pseudoizodom slabs over a rubble base covering an area

of bix 6.8 m. Its wall form. In height. The straight abastirus doorposts on two sides merged with a grand niche. The straight niche on its wall is sur surrounded by bull emports and is the sole ornament of the monument.

The fountain of Domitianus: This fountain, which faces the Domitianus square and has a water pool in front of it, and the Domitianus square with the monumental imperial concrete with fountain of the emperor Bassus (hydrekdokheion) which serves as the water distribution point for Ephesus. From the inscriptions this fountain was constructed in 92/93 A.D. The front of the fountain formed a large arch, decorated with two acanthus leaves on two sides and which was restored as two doorposts in a combination of concrete and marble. There was a space behind the front of the fountain, which resembled in shape a large apse. Among the

decorations of the fountain in the niche station in the middle (Exhibited in Chamber 2 of the Seljuk Museum of Ephesus), there were a group of statues that depicted the adventures of Odysseus and the Giant Polyphemos, which had been brought from another monument. The water brought from ... il by way of the Great ... water line, was distributed ... ernment Agora, from ... which is connected to the fountain of Laekanius Bassus (hydrekdokheion). It can be measured from the fact that the water line which continued from the Hydrekdokheion ended in this fountain and there are statues of the River Gods Marnas (displayed in The Seljuk Museum of Ephesus) and Klaseas in the north and south aediculas (small niches) and the statue of Zeus on the west aedicula, that this structure was a monumental fountain. It was repaired during the reign of Constantinus II

THE FOUNTAIN OF LAECANIUS BASSUS (HYDREKDOKHEION)

THE FOUNTAIN OF LAECANIUS BASSUS (HYDREKDOKHEION)

The fountain of Laecanius Bassus (mentioned in the inscriptions as Hydrekdokheion) was one of the large and highly ornamented two storey monumental structures of the city and was constructed by the Governor General C. Laecanius Bassus in 80-82 A.D. It stands between South Street, facing the Magnesia Gate via the South Stoa, and southwest of the Government Agora, facing Domitianus Street and the terrace. This is the oldest example of a monumental fountain in Ephesus. The water, which was brought via the Great Marnas water pipe from Mount Bülbül, was transmitted to the Government Agora through the Magnesia Gate and from there it was connected to this storage-fountain structure. The main pool that served as a water storage facility measuring 12.35 x 8.30 m. was surrounded by a two storey facade with aediculas. A pediment with five niches below was constructed on the rear face of the fountain, with decorations on the pediment that continued on the hypaethral wings to the sides. The statues on the upper level, positioned between two columns, give the structure a particular grandeur. On the lower level, in addition to various other statues, there are statues of both sea creatures and River Gods that spouted water into the pool.

THE TEMPLE OF DOMITIANUS

An impressive extensive area was established through the terracing of the hillside facing the southwest of Domitianus Street, the sides of this terraced area facing east and north to the square were supported by two-storey vaulted supports. The title of Neokoros (Guardian of the Temple), which was requested from the Roman Senate at the beginning of the 1st century A.D. and which was not granted, was finally given to the city by Emperor Domitianus. In order to show their gratitude for this honor, the people of Ephesus constructed this temple raised in honor of Emperor Domitianus (81-96 A.D.) and his wife. The temple of the Emperor of the Asia State in Ephesus, which is mentioned in inscriptions, is generally identified with this structure. The temple was first constructed in honor of Domitianus and his deified ancestors and, when Domitianus was killed, the Roman Senate decided to deem him damnatio memoriae (removed from memory). For this reason the people of Ephesus hid the head of the statue of Domitianus in the cellar of the temple and due to this judgement by the Roman Senate, the city of Ephesus was obliged to either demolish the temple that they constructed for Emperor Domitianus or lose the title of Neokoros, which they had managed to acquire after many difficulties after the passage of many years. In consequence, the torso of this statue was then completed with the carved head of Emperor Domitianus's father, Vespasianus, thereby transferring the title of Neokoros to his father, Vespasianus. In addition, the name of the Emperor Domitianus was erased from most of the inscriptions and was replaced by the name Vespasianus. In 1975, some fallen architectural parts of the facade were erected in a combination of marble and concrete, comprising statues of men and women as a support, over the lower level adorned with a roof of slabs, low vaults and half columns, resembling the Doric style (restoration). The terrace of the temple was approached from this porch by double stairs. This temple, constructed over a 6 stepped podium (24 x 34 m.), is pseudodipteros with an 8 x 13 columned peristasis. The ruins to the east of the temple indicate that there was a U shaped altar located on this podium. The podium, embellished with relief friezes depicting sacrificial rites and weapons, had a small porch (exhibited in the Museum of Ephesus). Later, architectural parts of the facade were collected and reused in Late Antiquity for the reconstruction of the Lower Agora, the Kuretes Street and the Theatre. After the establishment of Christianity as the official religion of the state this temple was demolished and the statues that embellished it were destroyed.

THE GATE OF HERCULES

In the Late Antique period a monumental gate was built from reused materials in the east corner of the Kuretes Street. This gate takes its name from its two doorposts which carry carved reliefs of Hercules and was constructed in the 5th century A.D., to control vehicles moving up the street. It is an arch which has an inscription over the doorposts which are decorated with depictions of Hercules wrapped in the fleece of the Nemean Lion. This structure can be dated to around the third quarter of the 5th century since the name Flavius Constantinus is written in the ruins of inscriptions over the archivolts (arch shaped supports). A corner block carries a relief of a flying Nike with a palm branch in the right hand and a garland made of leaves of daphne. The design of the Nike figure can be dated to the first half of the 4th century. Small repairs and modifications were later made to this gate.

KURETES STREET

This is one of the main streets of Ephesus, 210 m. long, that connects the Magnesia Gate to the Koresos Gate. This sacred path, earlier known as the Cortege Path of Artemis, had religious importance and it continued its existence contrary to the hippodamic system of the Hellenistic-Roman city. There is a 20 m. difference in height between the ends of Kuretes Street; which is why the Ephesus excursions begin from the upper end of this street. It was named Kuretes Street following the discovery of column tambours that had been taken from the Prytaneion and were reused in the entrance of this street, that carries the names of the Priests (Kuretes). This street, largely paved in marble, has in parts stone pavements and there is a deep drain pipe under the street.

Secondary roads connect to the Kuretes Street horizontally in accordance with the grid iron plan of the city. Mount Pion is connected to Kuretes Street by four narrow paths from its northern slope, two of which continue as alleys with stairs. These secondary roads are paved not only in limestone blocks, but also with a

small number of reused marbles and the drain pipes are connected to the main pipes of the city extending under this street. While there are columns on both sides in the large area on the upper section of the street which is paved with marble blocks, there are more public structures on the northern side of the Tetragonos Agora (including the Fountain of Traianus, the Bath of Varius and the Temple of Hadrianus) and there are tombs and monuments on its southern side. In addition to the monumental structures, statues of prominent people of the city were placed on the pedestals erected at the sides of this street and there are stoas with mosaics on both sides of the street. In places there are stores, shops, restaurants, taverns and spice stores behind these stoas and the small rooms behind these stores were used as workshops.

THE FOUNTAIN OF TRAIANUS

This is one of the three most magnificent fountains of Ephesus. It was erected to honor the Emperor Traianus in 114 A.D., and was 9.50 m. high and it continued the tradition of the theatre scene (skaenae frons) with its two storey statue of Emperor Traianus twice life-size. The architrave has on its upper face the insitu carved feet remaining from the original marble statue of Emperor Traianus. The sphere under Emperor Traianus' foot symbolizes the world and emphasizes world domination aspired to by Roman government. The pool was filled upper level and carry entablatures with pediments. The aedicula emphasized by a triangular pediment, horizontal volutes on the wings and corners of the rear facade, and the curved pediments in front of the wings facing the street. The niches in front of the fountain were decorated with statues of

columned front decorated with various statues. It is understood from the frieze and inscription on the architrave of the lower level that this fountain was constructed by Tiberius Claudius Aristion and was dedicated to Emperor Traianus. The two storey columned front of the Fountain of Traianus became more magnificent with the addition of two wings facing the façade on either side. A pool 11.90 m. long and 5.40 m. wide was constructed in front of the fountain between these two wings. In the middle section of the façade, a two storey niche was constructed. In the middle niche, there is a with the water that came from the pipes beneath the plinth. Some of the statues from here are in the British Museum, London others are in the Museum of Ephesus. There are composite capitals on the columns on the lower pedestals in front of the fountain. There were aediculas (small niches) between each of the columns on the sides. The columns on the upper level had octagonal pedestals and Corinthian capitals. Wall supports were placed on the rear facade of the structure according with the columns in front. The columns of the mid-section are wider on the (small niche) in the middle is Aphrodite, Dionysus, a young hunter figure which symbolizes the hunter figure which symbolizes the founder of the city, Androklos, Emperor Nerva, some women (portrait or with garments) and a reclining Satyr. This fountain was partially reconstructed after being heavily damaged by seismic activity, probably in the earthquake of 362 A.D. Other architectural parts of the fountain are displayed inside the pool and in front of it. In order to provide an indication of the visual quality of this fountain, it was partially rebuilt with concrete on a smaller scale than the original.

THE FOUNTAIN OF TRAIANUS

THE BATHS OF VARIUS (SCOLASTIKIA)

On the northern side of Kuretes Street are the Baths of Varius one of Ephesus's largest baths. It was constructed in the 1st century A.D. and was discovered during excavations conducted in 1926. It stands on a city block between Academia Street and Bath Street. In this bath complex near Kuretes Street, there is a small building called the Temple of Hadrianus and a large store. Bath Street which leads to the back of the theatre is 250 m. long and it is possible to enter these baths from this street. The plan of this bath house is typical of Roman bath architecture. From the gate in Bath Street, one enters the Bath of Varius and the chamber with an apse, including the dressing room and the entrance (apodyterium). There are niches on the walls. In on of these niches, there is a statue of Scolastika. The baths were repaired in 358 A.D. and 365 in the early Christian period. There is another entrance to the baths on the east of the Temple of Hadrianus and the stairs from Kuretes Street. From the Apodyterium, there are passages to the cold Frigidarium (Cold Section), a large Tepidarium (Warm Section), the Caldarium (Hot Section) and the Sudatorium (Sweating Section). Water, brought to the complex in clay pipes, was heated in the Praefurnium (furnace). At the same time, hot air from the Praefurnium provided the heat for the heated sections of the baths, passing through the hypocaust system under the floor and in the gap between the walls and the marble revetments covering the wall. Then this hot air was released through the chimneys.

THE TEMPLE OF HADRIANUS

In the pedestal mosaic of the gallery in front, mythological sea creatures are depicted (a Nereid mounting a seahorse of Triton). The most important room in residence No. 3 has depictions of the 9 Muses, and of Sappho and Apollo. Furthermore, the portraits, on the east wall of the inner court, depicting the renowned philosophers of the period, are of great importance for the history of art. In residence No. 4 are depictions of Socrates (today displayed in the Seljuk Museum of Ephesus) and the Muse Urania. By the door to the east section of the house are the frescoes belonging to the oldest period of decoration at Ephesus. The changes brought about through the construction of the apse of the basilica on the lower terrace destroyed the balance of this residence. Also the stairs provide a connection to residence No. 6, and it is thought that the owner of residence No. 4 was also the owner of this northern adjacent house. Due to the wealth of the owner, it was thought that in the period between the 2nd and 3rd centuries A.D., that residence No. 4 was used as the kitchen for

residence No. 6. Apart from the spaciousness of residence No. 6, of 950 m², the social, economic and religious duties and the home of an Ephesian notable during the reign of Emperor Severus was revealed through the finds made in the excavation of this residence. It is understood to have been more important than the other residences on the slope, as there is an inscription which indicates its owner at the end of the 2nd century A.D. was C. Flavius Furius Aptus and it is known that Furis Aptus, a notable of Ephesus, at least once at the end of the 2nd century A.D. had sponsored the Games held at Ephesus. This residence has a peristyle court, thought to have been of two

storeys. From this court one could enter the rooms in the west and north, a magnificent hall covered in marble on the south side, and the tunnel vaulted Private Basilica accessed from a small court with cross vaults in the southwest. The importance to the home owner of the Dionysus cult is also reflected in the decorations inside the house and the subjects of the plaster reliefs in the vaults of a small room which opens to the main court in a basilica style. The thiasos carrying creatures of Dionysus are depicted on the vaulted ceilings, which are divided geometrically while the

wedding of Dionysus and Ariadne among the Erotes is depicted on the stage by the pediment arch. Residence No. 7, of 900 m² was connected at times to residence No. 6 lying to its west. This residence, built according to the traditional plan, is full of rooms having differing characteristics, all surrounding the central inner court. There are marble effigies of Emperor Augustus' wife Livia and his sons, and Emperor Tiberius with a bronze statue of a snake (displayed in the Museum of Ephesus) in the peristyle exedra on the southern side.

THE OCTAGON AND THE FOUNTAIN OF THE CITY-FOUNDER ANDROKLOS

The Octagon: is located by the side of Kuretes Street on the northwestern corner of the second Slope House. This building, which has inscriptions in Latin and Greek on the side facing the street, is a monumental tomb for Cleopatra's sister Arsinoe IV, who was killed in 41 B.C. and is of an octagonal shape on top of a pedestal of a tetragonal shape.There is a vault and a sarcophagus in this building. This octagonal building is surrounded by columns. The parts close to the roof are embellished with garlands and the roof was of a conical shape. The parts belonging to the roof and the Corinthian capitals of the tomb are still preserved. "The division of the monetary help to the cities after the earthquake", is recorded in the Latin inscription on the left side. The inscription on the right side in Latin and Greek is about, "providing the funding for the State Festival Games by the four cities".

The Fountain of the City-Founder Androklos: It is a fountain building constructed in honor of Androklos, the mythological founder of Ephesus and is situated in the north of Kuretes Street, close to its end. The upper level is in the Ionic order and the lower level in the Doric order. The roof reliefs and frieze pieces found in the excavations indicate that the building was constructed in the 2nd century B.C. The water source called Hypelaia is inside this building complex. Its facade was covered with marble in the Byzantine period and so this fountain is also called the Byzantine Fountain.

THE LATRINA (PUBLIC LAVATORY)

In Ephesus every need was considered; a latrina (a public lavatory) was built at the corner of Kuretes Street and the Academy Path, facing the baths of Varius. On three sides of the open peristyle court are U-shaped marble seats with holes (toilet seats). A deep sewage pipe was located under the seats allowing for the fast sterilization of the toilet drains and

the rapid removal of bad smells. The clean water passing through the channels in front of the toilet seats gave the people the means to clean themselves up. Rain water was also passed from the channels beneath the Latrina in the connected pipes. In this place people lifted the togas they wore and could use the facilities in a group at the same time. The floor was paved with mosaics around the pool in the middle.

THE LOVE HOUSE

The house next door to the latrina has figured mosaic pavements and, together with the inscription of

Parthiskelon on the reused architrave, are evidence this building was called the "Love House". It was constructed in the 1st century A.D. and renewed after the earthquake in the 4th century A.D. This building contains lots of rooms and halls around a court. When entered from the Marble Street one saw a two-stage pool. There was an entrance from the left side of this pool to a court surrounded by four rooms. The two front Korinthos ... The upper level in the Ionic order and the lower level in the Doric order. The reliefs and frieze pieces found in the excavations indicate that the building was constructed in the 2nd were paved with mosaics. Three women drinking and sitting around a table are depicted in the floor mosaics of the small room. It indicates that the two women's rooms were on the ... The rooms on the ground floor were reserved for the guests. The portraits of four women are depicted in the mosaic in the dining room with the four seasons of the year described through the depiction of these ...

four women in the ... this house. The most significant indications that this house was ... Below the inscription found in the Latrina, this inscription was used in the ... century B.C. The water called Hypelaia is inside the building complex. ... It was covered with marble in the Byzantine period and ... this fountain is decorated ...

house in this ... portraying the ... with a ... and numerous ... some of which are ... Museum of Ephesus. ... is also ... an arrow and a ... of a woman ... marble block, which also ... indicate a connection ... ... love house and ... effigy of the woman "Polo" indicates the library. It reads ... ... the installation.

THE LIBRARY OF CELSUS

THE LIBRARY OF CELSUS

The library building, which is located on the corner of the west side of Kuretes Street and the southwestern side of the South Gate of the Tetragonos Agora, was constructed on the tetragonal area acquired after the demolition of half of the peristyle house in the south of the center. The library building was discovered during the excavations of 1905-1906. The facade of the library was restored between 1970 and 1978 by the Excavations Directorate, reusing the original materials, as well as employing modern materials substituted for the missing pieces according to its original appearance. The marble sarcophagus of Celsus, who died in Rome aged 70 in 114 A.D. when he was the Governor of Asia Minor, was put into the tomb by the southern entrance of the Tetragonos Agora. Before his death, Celsus bequeathed 25.000 dinars and requested the construction of a library and the purchase of new books for the library every year with the interest on the remaining money. There were initially 12.000 books in this library. The library was constructed by Celsus Julius Aquila as a heroon on the tomb of the Roman Senator Tiberius

Julius Celsus Polemaeanus in the 1st quarter of the 2nd century A.D. The precise information provided by the inscriptions on the pedestals on two sides of the stairs indicates that Tiberius Julius Celsus Polemaeanus, who was probably from Sardis, was the Consul in 92 A.D. and the Proconsul of Asia in 106-107, and information about his public service and social status. Furthermore it is recorded in the recovered inscriptions that, "the library was constructed by the son of Celsus and the Consul in 110 A.D., Celsus Julius Aquila, for his father as a heroon". The library was entered through the three gates which were located symmetrical to the axis on the facade with aediculas (small niches) reached by stairs of 9 steps and with statue pedestals on both sides. The indented design of the two-storied alive-like facade of the library was achieved through the architectural elements overlapping on the upper and lower levels. Being narrower, the lower level had four higher aediculas while the upper level had three wider aediculas. There were single columns carrying detached entablatures on both sides. The windows on the upper level accord with the entrances on the lower level through the plan of the

facade designed by the architects of the library, a beguiling perspective was created and the audience was mislead into thinking that the stage was wider than it actually was, through giving a curve to the horizontal elements of the building and increasing by a certain proportion the vertical elements of the construction on the central axis. Even though the front of the library was two-storied, the building inside was three-storied. The reading hall behind the facade was constructed following a tetragonal plan and the floor pavements and wall panels were covered by marble plaques of various colors. There was an apse in the rear wall of the library and there was a statue of the Goddess Athena within this grand niched arch. There was the marble sarcophagus of Tiberius Julius Celsus Polemaeanus beneath the apse and the vault was reached through a narrow passage in the north of the library. There were two storeys above the reading hall in the entrance, which was where

the books were kept. The books, rolled scrolls (generally of papyrus) were kept in the niches in these two floors and were accessed from the galleries.
As a result of the severe earthquakes in 262 A.D. the reading hall of the library caught fire and was destroyed and the main hall was not restored.
A pool was constructed on the stairs of the library with large scale carved relief plates, and the front of the library provided the magnificent rear wall of this pool during the Late Antique period. The large scale circular relief plaques on the front of the fountain which were known as the "Plaques of Parth".
These originally formed parts of the monumental altar constructed in honor of Emperor Lucius Verus in the mid-2nd century. Today most of these plaques are in the Museum of Ephesus in Vienna, with the recently discovered pieces exhibited in the Museum of Ephesus in Seljuk. The front of

the Library was completely destroyed by an earthquake in the Middle Ages.

THE GATES OF MA-ZAEUS AND MITHRIDATES

This was at the end of Kuretes Street, by the southern gate of the northern agora in the Library Court, which was called Triodos in antiquity. It was first constructed as a triumphal arch but then after the reign of Emperor Augustus was converted into the entrance gate of the Agora. Between 1979 and 1988 the missing parts of the gate, which was still in part standing, were restored and completed with modern replacement parts by the Excavations Directorate.
Both Mazaeus and Mithridates were slaves of Emperor Augustus and his heir Agrippa. Emperor Augustus set them free and sent them to Ephesus as officers in

charge of maintaining the properties belonging to the Roman Empire in Ephesus. Mazaeus and Mithridates constructed this monumental gate in appreciation of their former owners: it was constructed in 3 B.C. in honor of Emperor Augustus, his wife Livia, his son-in-law Agrippa who had died and his daughter Julia. The inscription on this building is in two languages. It was written in full detail in Latin on the sides of the Attica and an extract in Greek was placed in the middle section at the back. The inscription in Latin on the left records that it was former masters of Mithridates and the people". The monumental gate of Mazaeus and Mithridates consisted of three arched gates. These arched gates ended by the side of the Tetragonos Agora in the same line, whereas the middle facade of the arched gate of the Library Agora was slightly recessed. The gates were connected to each other by richly decorated doorposts. There are two round niches in the outer walls. The roof of the gate consisted of an architrave in three ornamented sections, a frieze adorned with vines and a dentil this place. Further, all the walls of the gate were filled with notices concerning the grain supply to the city, price announcements, orders concerning other issues and environmental plans. The original appearance of the northern front of the gate was ruined during the course of modifications carried out in the 1st century A.D. According to a notice, in order to prevent rainwater running down Kuretes Street from overflowing into the Agora, the ground level of the South Gate was raised, to let the water accumulate in the channels.

constructed for "the son of Caesar, Augustus, who was chosen for the 20th time as the perfect head of the people's assembly, the 12th time as Consul and High Priest, and his wife Livia" and, on the right, that it was constructed for, "the son of Lucius, Agrippa, who was chosen for the 6th time as the perfect emperor of the people's assembly, the 3rd time as Consul, Julia, daughter of Caesar Augustus, the border. The attica on the entablature with the inscription was bordered by a cornice molding on the top and interlaced moulding on the bottom. There were the statues of the family of the Emperor on the attica. There is a relief of Hecate, the God responsible for crossroads on the outer walls of the gate. On the architrave on the southeastern niche are curses on those people who choose to relieve themselves in There were two storied wing structures on both sides of the gate, probably containing the tombs of Mazaeus and Mithridates, when it was first constructed. The eastern wing was pulled down during the modifications made to the Agora and the western wing, which contained the tomb of Mazaeus, was pulled down, at the latest when the library was constructed.

THE TETRAGONOS AGORA

This was the trade area recorded as the "Tetragonos Agora" in the written sources. The condition of the Agora in the Late Antique period was revealed during excavations in 1901-1907 during excavations in the plain to the west of the Marble Street. Traces of the Hellenistic Agora were found 3 m. below the present ground level during deep excavations in the Agora in 1977. The Hellenistic Agora was only half as large as the Roman Agora. It is thought from the architectural pieces recovered from the excavations that the remains of a storage building with two rows of rooms stood on the southwestern corner of the Agora and the stoa which lay at the end of the road next to the Western Gate, were constructed successively in the 3rd and 2nd centuries B.C. during the reign of Lysimachus. The Agora had rectangular rooms around its sides and theserooms at the end of the 1st century B.C. were widened to form rooms square in shape (measuring 112 x 112 m.). It had three monumental gates, two galleries on four sides and was a closed court surrounded by stoas. Most of these rooms were used for mercantile purposes, although some were the meeting places for guilds and political associations. The traces of stairs found in the corner of the Southeastern Agora next to the Western Gate and to the east of the Northern Gate prove that these stoa were two-storied buildings. The Agora was devastated by earthquakes in the 3rd and the 4th century A.D., and was reconstructed by Emperor Theodosius I. (379-395 A.D.) according to its original plan, with reused materials, which is why it is also known as the "Theodosius Forum". It continued to function as an agora until the 7th century A.D.

The Western Gate: This was the main entrance to the Agora, raised on a large podium (17 m.) at the end of the avenue leading from the harbor to the city (the West Street). There were double columns on the wings on both sides of the front and ten-stepped flight of steps and two side-rows of columns in the back. There are rich decorations on the pedestals, some of which remain in their original locations and the Ionic capitals surrounding the gates are noteworthy. On both sides of the gate there were marble benches for people to sit. This monumental Western Gate was constructed on the foundations of a smaller Augustan Gate following the earthquake of 23 A.D. In the period of Domitianus (81-96 A.D.) a merchant from Alexandria made alterations to the gate, which was not then suitable for freight traffic. The present condition of the Gate can be connected to these first alterations made in antiquity, three gates in the entrance building, two large water pools and loading ramps at the sides for heavily loaded vehicles. The large court of the Agora was decorated with numerous statues and altar monuments, the foundations of which remain today in their original positions.

THE WEST GATE OF AGORA

37

THE STOA OF NERO

The Stoa of Nero was located east of the Agora. It was a basilica of two naves, which extended beside the Marble Street for 150 meters. This stoa was dedicated to "Artemis of Ephesus, Nero and his mother Agrippina and the people of Ephesus", as recorded in its inscription and was called the Stoa of Nero. The terrace wall of the Stoa of Nero facing Marble Street was faced with bossed masonry blocks and was 1.70 m. above street level. The main gate in the south of the basilica was entered from the stairs in the Library Agora. The western nave of the Stoa of Nero, which was constructed on the rooms of the eastern stoa of the Agora, was completely demolished and consequently there is no precise information concerning the appearance of the stoa facade facing the Agora and whether it had a connection to the main stoa adjacent to it on its western side.

THE MARBLE STREET

Kuretes Street ended at the corner of the Library Agora. The Marble Street started from the side of the Library Agora, passed from the eastern corner of the Tetragonos Agora and reached the Theatre Court without spoiling the integrity of the street. This was the main street of Ephesus during the Empire period and it was at the same time the primary religious ceremonial (processional) street and this street was completely paved in marble. There were stoas for pedestrians along both sides of this street, along which vehicles passed. The main sewage pipes passing under Kuretes Street at the Library Court divided into two, with one section continuing to the Western Gate beneath the Tetragonos Agora, the other running beneath the Marble Street. There was the Stoa of Nero on the western side of the city and another stoa which ended by the analemma wall at the northern side of the grand theatre to the east. There were one-room lodgings employed for trade purposes behind the columns of the eastern stoa and there were the entrances of the humble and multistoried residences, only few of which have been excavated. The Stoa of Nero extending along the western side of the Marble Street, was elevated 1.70 m. above street level and there was an arched entrance gate near its northern edge. The terrace wall of the Stoa of Nero was constructed with bossed masonry blocks.

There was a depiction of a heart punctured with an arrow and a foot, and an effigy of a woman of Polos engraved on a marble block that were found close to the middle of the stoa. The depiction of the heart indicates the love house and the effigy of the woman of Polos indicates the library as noted above is related by some. In later periods this street intersected with the city walls adjacent to the rear wall of the theatre stage building where a "city gate" with grand marble doorposts was constructed from reused blocks. Widening out behind this gate, the street continued to the Arkadiane and to the Theatre Court, where large stairs provided entry to the theatre.

THE GRAND THEATRE

As in all ancient city theatres, the theatre of Ephesus had its seats on the slopes (of Mount Pion). This great city of Anatolia had one of the grand theatres of Anatolia constructed to accommodate 25.000 people after the modifications made to it during the council, public unions and the meetings of theologians.

The date when the theater was first constructed is unknown. However, the presence of the theatre in the Hellenistic period is known from the erection of a small fountain (the Hellenistic Fountain) in the northwestern corner of the stage structure, dating from around 100 B.C. Further this relates to the probable date of foundation of the Asian state of Anatolia in 133 B.C. Initially the first structure was a small and simple stage and then of Nero. The orchestra was also expanded by adding a low proskenion (front stage) for the orchestra and a logeion on the stage of the theatre. In this period a second series of seating benches were constructed on top of the

Roman Imperial period. It stands on the sacred route between the Magnesia Gate and the Koresos Gate. Theatres were significant centers in urban life and the assembly places of ancient cities, of great importance to the social structure of the city because the theatres not only displayed presentations and artistic contests, but also various assemblies such as the council of the elders, the youth orchestra, which used to be a water channel, with a seating bench surrounding this structure. In the Augustan period came the rapid expansion of the city of Ephesus and, parallel to the expansion of the city, the theatre was also increased in size. A richly decorated storey was added to the stage between 87 and 92 A.D. from the inscriptions following the construction boom during the rule of Domitianus and vaulted foundations adjacent to the analemmata (side walls). The seating benches were divided with a cross-wise broad path (diazoma) and the upper seating benches were accessed through the stairs from this diazoma. The lowest seating benches were divided by narrow stairs into individual seating sections called kerkides, forming 11 wedge shaped areas. The number of stairs providing

access was doubled in the second and the third seating sections, forming 21 kerkides in each. The seating sections of the first level reached 19, the second level 20 and the third level 23. There were stone seats (prohedria) on the second diazoma, which was wider, for the directors of the plays and for the judges of the contests that were held in the theater.

We learn from the inscriptions the sections of the theater in which each of the following city bodies sat as a group: the city council (boule) (the municipality assembly), gerousia (the council of the elderly), phyle (the clans), the theologes (the lecturers of ceremonies) etc.). According to one of the architrave inscriptions, the third seating section was accessed by the stairs constructed on broad and high vaults and which was finished a little after 100 A.D. One of the long inscriptions in the theatre records that a person named C. Vibius Salutaris made a generous

donation to the religious rites in 104 A.D. and he had made the silver statues of Artemis and Emperor Traianus that were displayed during public assemblies. It is known from the inscriptions that the sunshade, which was installed in the theatre in the middle of the 2nd century A.D., was repaired in 205-240 A.D. Above the second seating section there was a kind of tribune (a sacred area dedicated to Nemesis, the God of Contests), which was on the uppermost level of the theatre and had a line of columns in the front, and the 3rd seating section, which was situated on the in-part higher vaulted structures. A second diazoma separated the second and the third seating sections. The third seating section was entered through the stairs from the diazoma and from the stairs, constructed with broad and high vaults, in the analemma wall from outside the theatre known, but it is thought to have been before 262 A.D. It is understood from the murals on the stage wall that after the great earthquake in 262 A.D. most of the theatre was destroyed, the top section of the analemma was never used again and a more populist approach to public entertainment ensued, such as violent games and gladiatorial fights, instead of the former repertory of classical theatre entertainment. Further, the theatre was again damaged by earthquakes in 359 and 366 A.D., and was then altered through being included within the defense system constructed in the 8th century. Its current appearance is the result of the repairs that were made to it during the Late Antique period. According to the Bible, Demetrios argued against the Christian disciple Paulos (Paul) in this theatre and made the Ephesians chant "Artemis of Ephesians is the greatest". Sometimes concerts were held in this theatre at night.

THE HELLENISTIC FOUNTAIN

The fountain is by the side of the Theatre Court, north of the stage structure. It is the best preserved Hellenistic work of art in Ephesus. It was constructed from marble blocks and the side walls of the fountain were turned into anta walls and completed with anta capitals. Two fluted columns with Ionic capitals were placed between the anta walls as supports. There was an architrave with fascia over the capitals. The architrave carried a dentil border and the line of the cornice on the exterior and a slabbed marble roof on the inside. In the inscription on one of the columns it is recorded that the, "water here was brought from Great Marnas River". The water, brought via pipes, poured into the pool through the three lion heads on the marble rear wall. The front of the fountain is simply decorated, with only the Ionic capitals. This fountain erected by the side of an important court of the city must have been decorated with paintwork, as was the case for many other structures. During the Roman period, this simple Hellenistic structure was extended by 2 meters to the front and two columns were added to its porch facing the road.

THE ARKADIANE (HARBOR STREET)

This marble street that extends from the theater to the harbor is 11 meters wide and 525 meter long (equal to 1.800 foot of Byzantium). This street was an important structure of the city, as since the Early Roman period many kings, emperors, councils from other cities and merchants coming by sea to Ephesus were officially greeted here. There is also a sewage channel under this street which comes from the Marble Street and extends to the harbor. This street established in the Early

... was named after ... Evangelios of 395-366 A.D by emperor Arkadius (395-408 A.D) ... and thus was ... rebuilt. It is known that it was street lighting on the each lane in the 5th century A.D. This street ... ... ends in another direction. In 6th century A.D. there was a structure in the middle of the street, constructed of four ... columns, situated ... on square pedestals with ... The 2 m. high circular ... pedestals adorned with the symbols of Christianity are decorated with niches and columns on the sides. There are column postaments, a grand column and a

column capital on top of the circular postament Column; there were statues of four Evangelists on top of these four column capitals. Thus the Christianity of the Ephesians was demonstrated to visitors to the city who arrived at the harbor.

THE ARKADIANE (HARBOR STREET)

THE THEATRE GYMNASIUM

This is the Bath-Gymnasium structure lying north of the Theatre Court, at the beginning of Arcadius Street. It has a 70 x 30 m. palaestra (wrestling) court surrounded on three sides by stoa, whose podiums were covered in marble. A tribune, consisting of four rows of seating stairs was constructed on the northern side of the Gymnasium. A slightly pitched area was added to the tribune, constructed for the standing audience on the side facing the Baths. Because it was very close to the theatre and its palaestra had a stadium, this structure is thought to have been used to train the theatre actors; and in consequence it was named "The Theatre Gymnasium". There was a bath complex just behind the tribune north of the Gymnasium. The excavation of this baths has begun but remains incomplete. There were lines of rooms on the southern and northern sides of this bath complex. The rooms on the southern side of the Bath were dressing rooms (Apodyterium); a hot bathing section (Calidarium) and hot water pools. These rooms were slightly larger than the other rooms, which were in the middle of the Baths. The Bath had a long U-shaped area (warm section – Tepidarium), which was for recreation and visiting, in the outer area of the northern and southern rooms of the Bath. The second U shaped area inside the Baths was called the cold section (Frigidarium) and in the middle section there was a swimming pool (Natatio). The Bath was heated through the hot air that circulated under the paved floor; the system termed a "Hypocaust".

THE CHURCH OF MARY

The small path on the right side of the exit gate of Ephesus leads you to the Church of Mary. In the 4th century A.D., a church complex 145 m. long was constructed on the western side of the Southern Stoa of Olympieion. It was the first church to be constructed in the name of the Virgin Mary. This church was used as an educational center for Ephesian Christian clergymen. The church and the additions made to it were constructed on top of an already extant long structure. According to an inscription here, this structure had for a long time been a school of medicine, although some archeologists think this structure was not the school of medicine but was a basilica of three naves. The church that was dedicated to

Mary underwent many phases of construction. In the first construction phase there were an atrium, resembling a peristyle, where the pedestals were covered with inscriptions dating from the Roman Imperial period, a cross-wise narthex and a three naved church, with the middle nave supported by 40 columns on the west side of the church. On the east edge of the middle nave there was a large apse, constructed of ashlar masonry from the Roman stoa. There were pastophorion chambers on both sides of the apse, where ritual objects were stored. On the northern side of the atrium there was a niched baptistery of octagonal shape with a baptism chamber covered in marble resembling a "tholos", and a pool was added to this structure, constructed in the middle of the floor for the baptism of adults. The

church, which was demolished in the earthquakes of 557 A.D., was then rebuilt with great changes. In this second phase, the eastern part of the church, whose columns were removed and separated in the middle, was turned into a basilica with a narrow narthex and columns. The western part of the church was rebuilt in a very different way. The church constructed of bricks had narrow side-naves, a low vault supported by elephant feet and a dome over the middle nave. There were pastophorions on both sides of the apse end, appearing like chapels next to the middle nave. An inner narthex (ezonarthex) was added to the western side; consequently a collection of religious buildings were erected, the eastern side was given to the Bishop, the western side to the congregation. The Bishop's Church was used until it

was sacked by Muslim raiders in 654/5. However, it is understood from the doors opening to the apse of the brick church that it served as a graveyard until the 11th century and there was a graveyard on the northern side until the 14th century, so this area didn't entirely lose its function and association with Christianity. It began being used as a graveyard during the second construction phase in the second half of the 6th century. From research it is known that only the Bishops were buried in the narthex on the eastern side. Later a large graveyard was created, not only inside the brick structure but also on the outside. The continued use of this cemetery into the 14th century shows the Christians were able to continue using their sanctuaries in Ephesus, even after Ephesus came under the rule of the Aydınoğulları Emirate.

On the 22nd of June 431 a Council gathered in this church and 195 Bishops participated in this Council where, amongst other issues, the divine and human nature of Jesus Christ was discussed, and it is certain that the Church of Ephesus, which earned a good reputation for housing the deliberations of this Ecumenical Council, was the Church of Mary. At this Council the question as to whether Mary was the Mother of God or not was put forward for discussion and the Bishop of Constantinople (Istanbul), Nestorius, stirred up a hornet's nest and was excommunicated when he said that Jesus Christ was not the son of God but merely a good man. The Patriarch of Alexandria, Cyrillus (Cyril), defended the understanding that Jesus Christ had one personality but two entities and that Mary was actually the Mother of God. In conclusion, the views of Cyrillus were favored and the theology that stated Jesus Christ had a divine form and Mary was the Mother of God were confirmed by this Ecumenical Council. Recent research indicates the Christian structures were constructed in this place after 431 and that the whole of the Council or just a part of it may have taken place in the adapted stoa; as at that time this was not yet the Church of Mary. The Council records, compiled at a considerably later date, that indicate the Council gathered in a place called the Church of Mary, conflict with the archaeological evidence and this will only be resolved after the thorough examination of the latest philological and archeological evidence. [In 1967 Pope Paul IV, who visited Ephesus, prayed in this church.]

THE HARBOR BATHS

This grand complex, In the north of Arkadiane Street, consisted of a bath, a gymnasium and a sports area. It was planned symmetrically along an east-west axis. Construction started in the period of Domitianus; it was reconstructed after earthquake damage in 262 A.D. and it was finally completed in the 4th century A.D. "Atrium termarum Constantianarum" is recoded on an inscription here, which is why this baths is called the "Baths of Constantius". There is an entrance into a monumental court dating from Late Antiquity from the three-gate entrance in Arkadiane Street. Opposite the entrance to the south is an exedra adorned with statues. A pool was constructed in front of the exedra in Late Antiquity. There is a 45 m. entrance section in front of the bath.

This structure was surrounded on three sides by a peristyle with mosaic pedestals. A large quantity of reused marble was employed in the pavement of the court. The relief elements of the Monument of Parth were amongst the reused materials. The stairs on the northern side, with two wreathed columns, opened into a hall. Right next to the stairs there was a fountain basin decorated with bull capitals on top and garlands between them. The atrium by the side of the door has a three-naved plan. The outer walls of the atrium were separated into sections by brick pillars. The atrium provided entrance to the bath section to the north and the bath section was arranged symmetrically. There were three long spaces in the east of the bath. In the middle section there was the cold section (Frigidarium) with a huge, cold water pool (Natatio) inside and there were the

adjacent rooms for dressing and resting (Apodyterium). There was an entrance from the cold section into the warm section (Tepidarium), and to the three central chambers amongst the nine in the middle section of the bath. The hot section (Caldarium) was a large chamber, which stood on an outer ledge on the western front of the bath. It had large windows facing west and six hot water pools in the niches on the wall. The three chambers on both sides of the warm section (Tepidarium) were used for ball games, boxing, gymnastics, cosmetic work, body care and massage. The large number of insitu fixing elements on the walls and the floors of the chambers indicates they were covered by marble revetments. The bath was heated with hot air circulating under the pavement, termed a "Hypocaust".

THE TEMPLE OF SERAPEION

The Temple of Serapeion was located in a temenos in the foothills of Mount Bülbül to the west of the Tetragonos Agora. The temenos of the temple was surrounded with two-storey columns and was on a terrace orientated in a north-south direction built on top of Late Hellenistic structures at the beginning of the 2nd century A.D., in part carved into the bedrock and in part upon infill material.

As no inscription was found in the excavations, to which particular god this temple was dedicated is not certainly known. It was first called a Monumental Fountain (Nymphaion), then the Temple of Claudius; however in 1926 it was called the Serapeion and from that date it has been referred to by this name. In the 2nd century it was constructed as a temple resembling a pro-style with podiums and was devastated in the fire that broke out during the earthquake in the 4th century A.D.; and was then converted into a small church during the reign of Emperor Theodosius I. It stood on an eight columned porch, a landing and stairs of two levels. One-piece columns, 14-15 m. high carried Corinthian column capitals. It had three entrances below its richly ornamented pediment. The main entrance to the temple was on the narrow side in the north; but the temple could also be entered through the magnificent stairs from West Street. Beginning in Late Antiquity other stairs from the southwestern side of the Agora provided direct entrance to the temple. There were six small niches on the long wall of the Naos and there were small niches on both sides of the large niche in the middle of the southern wall that held the religious statue. Water channels passed beneath the niches on the inner walls of Naos. The water flowing from the vertical cracks in the large niches was led out via the channel in the floor. The extensive use of water in this temple indicates worship in the temple was connected to a Goddess of Health. There were five niches outside the Naos walls The trace remains of two bronze statues found during the excavations on the northeastern side of the temenos show this temple endowed with rich decorations. The rear wall of the stoa, at least on the ground floor, was covered in marble panels, positioned in accordance with the columns in the front and was divided into sections by wall supports which had postaments with reliefs and Corinthian capitals.

THE STADION

It was situated on the northwestern foothills of Mount Pion (Panayır Dağı) on the path leading to Seljuk from the Koresos gate of Ephesus. When first constructed there was seating on the southern hillside, a running course in front and a Hellenistic apse on its western side. The Roman Stadium was constructed by C. Stertinius Orpex, a freed slave, during the reign of the Roman Emperor Nero (54-68 A.D.) and it was then transformed into a monumental structure with aid from a foundation. While the Stadium was being turned into a monumental structure, a very large chamber, a vaulted infrastructure and seating benches on top were added facing the seating benches on the southern side. There were interior stairs leading to this seating area. The high northern front, constructed of ashlar masonry, had a monumental appearance. The arched gates of the magnificent western front led to the tunnels beneath the seating benches. Beside the running course there were bossed orthostatic panels and the track had a floor of pressed earth and was approximately 180 m. long and the stadium could hold 30.000-people. It is not certainly known how the elliptical area (sphendonc= pit area) leading to the corner in the east was used during its first phase. Athletics, chariot races and gladiatorial games were held in the Stadium. After the earthquake of 262 A.D., even though the southern gate and the western side were repaired, it is thought that the Stadium was greatly damaged after the earthquakes of 356 and 366. In the 5th century a church on the western end of the northern tunnel was added, only the entrance atrium was exposed in excavations and a graveyard was created around this church. This late phase of use continue at least until the 12th century.

THE CAVE OF ST. PAUL

Around 1900 the cave in the foothills of Mount Bülbül at a height of 100 m. to the north of the Temple of Serapeion was found by O. Benndorf. The cave of St. Paul was made by being roughly carved into the bedrock; producing an approximately 15 m. long aisle and a slightly larger chamber. Today the chamber, whose floors have been flattened and joined by steps, can be entered from the aisle decorated with reused materials. There are two niches of different sizes on the landing on the southern side of the aisle. The larger niche on the right side of the entrance reached the ground; but was only roughly and irregularly carved. The arches and aisle walls were covered in many layers of plaster. There was an antique panel carrying carvings of various prayers beneath the 20th century plaster of the uppermost layer. On this panel are invocations to St. Paul and "God, please help your disciple Timotheos!" During the conservation and restoration work in 1998 the murals depicting stories from the life of St. Paul and St. Thekla were found.

THE CAVE OF THE SEVEN SLEEPERS

The modern path, leading out from the city walls, leads to the Cave of the Seven Sleepers on Mount Pion (Panayır Dağı). According to written accounts, this is the place where seven young men and their dog came to after running away from the city because of the persecution of Christians during the reign of Emperor Decius (249-251 A.D.) and after falling asleep, they woke up 200 years later during the reign of Emperor Theodosios II. When these seven men and their dog woke up after the passage of 200 years, Christianity had become the official religion of Rome. The same story is also known and believed by Muslims (it is related in the 18th Sura of the Holy Koran). This account has been associated with many other caves in Anatolia. The next most important of these other caves of the Seven Sleepers was the sacred cave at Arabissos in

Cappadocia. The cave which is thought to be the place of the 5th ... during the reign of ... They built ... and this ... archeological ... traces of ... The church ... these ... via stairs in ... the front ... church had a main ... hes and mosaic ... built-in benches ... a synthronus, ... bishop and his ... and an apsed ... with an altar. There was a ... and covered crypt on the west side of the church. When the crypt became full, various new crypts were constructed of brick and about 700 of these crypts were found here. The cave, which was accepted as the site of the cave of the seven sleepers by Christians, has been visited not only by Christians but also by Muslim pilgrims since the Middle Ages.

THE ARTEMISION (THE TEMPLE OF ARTEMIS)

53

THE ARTEMISION (THE TEMPLE OF ARTEMIS)

The Temple of Artemis, considered to be one of the Seven Wonders of the World by ancient writers, was situated by the marshes to the southwest of Ayasuluk Hill. Its first construction was by the seaside. However this temple that stood by the seashore is today 5 km. inland, due to the alluvial infilling of the bay. Today there remains a 14 m. high column (its original height was 18.40 m) in the northeast, which was erected in 1973 with the aid of pulleys, an archaic column pedestal, a part of which can be seen, and a pedestal dating from the Late Classical period, which stood insitu right above the column. On the western side, the court walls of the Archaic temple, the point where the doorposts were attached, the traces of the Archaic marble stylobates, the southern anta in the classical covering of the Archaic temple, the west and north edges of the Archaic and Late Classical temples and the foundations of the hekatompedos can still today be seen. The structures connected with the foundations of the stairs leading to the platform of the Late Classical temple from the western court, the structures in the south of the foundations of the hekatompedos (naiskos, channel, road and the apsed structure) and the Archaic and Late Classical altar foundations can be seen. In the excavation area covered with ground water, from time to time earlier structures in the court, the traces of Temple C., the naiskos of the Temple of Kroisos and the cella walls of the peripteros can be seen but this depends upon the level of the water within this excavated area.

According to Strabo this temple had been repeatedly ruined and reconstructed. It was one of the Seven Wonders of the ancient world. The oldest traces of the temple, which underwent many construction phases, date from the 8th century B.C. This first temple was a peripteros planned structure with 4 columns on its short sides and 8 columns on its long sides. In this peripteros, the tetragonal platform surrounded by 6 columns functioned as the pedestal (baldaken) for the religious statue. From this earliest structure only the pedestals of green schist that supported the

wooden columns were found during the excavations. This temple was believed to have been ravaged by the Cimmerians. The dipterous plan of the magnificent Temple of Hera in Samos made the Ephesians jealous and it was then that they decided to construct a temple more magnificent than the Temple of Hera at Samos. Herodotus indicates this structure was called the Temple of Kroisos because of the financial and moral support of the Lydians including the columns that were donated by Kroisos during the construction of this Temple. Around 560 B.C. the construction of the first great marble dipterous began on the east-west axis, known to have been the Temple of Kroisos. The architects of the Archaic temple were

from Samos, Theodoros, Metagenes and Khersiphron. The Temple was situated in the marshes and in order to create foundations in this marshy ground the recommendation of the most prominent Samian artist, architect and sculptor, Theodoros, to put wood charcoal and fleece under the foundations (temeun), was followed and traces of charcoal and ash remains were found in the excavations. The foundations were created by putting big slates on these chunks of charcoal. Above this layer, polygonal marble panels, which constituted the surface of the Stylobate, were bonded and the floor of the temple was created, measuring approximately 55 x 115 m. Each of the columns (approximately 106 in number) were adorned with carved patterns on their lower sections (Columnae Caelatae), with the load system on the Stylobate carrying the weight, each section weighing more

than 100 tons, with the marble roof pediments carrying carved figurines and with carved marble roof tiles. However this roof didn't cover the whole of the temple but only covered the peristyle. The inner area, called the Sekos, was open to the sky and this was where the covered structure containing the religious statue in the naos was kept. The construction of this 6th century temple, that which is considered to have been one of the Seven Wonders of the World, lasted for 120 years. However in 356 B.C. it was burned down by someone who wanted through this action to immortalize his own name, Herostratos and this layer of fire damage was found during the excavations. After the temple was burnt, the Ephesians began the reconstruction of the temple. The architects of the new temple were Paionios, Demetrios and Kheirokrates. In the 4th century B.C. due to the rising sea level, a platform was constructed to prevent the ground water from flooding the temple. Another line of columns was added to this high structure with stairs. In addition an opisthodomos was added to the west facing rear side of the temple for the protection of the gifts that were donated to the Goddess Artemis. Thus there were three lines of 9 columns in the rear by the short sides and three lines of 8 columns in the front facing west. When observed from the sides, it had 21 columns on each side in two rows. This temple had in total 117 columns. In the depictions of the temple on coins, a door in the roof was observed and it is said this door was made and functioned as the place through which the Goddess Artemis watched the sacrifices that were made in her honor. According to the writings of Plinius (Pliny), the columns of this Hellenistic Temple of Artemis were 18.40 m. high. When Alexander the Great visited Ephesus, he offered to help in the construction of the temple and requested that an inscription with his name be put in the temple.

Thus Alexander the Great would be famous, just like Kroisos was with his temple. However the proud Ephesians politely turned down his offer, flatteringly replying to his offer with the words "One God cannot give presents to another". Despite this reply, Alexander the Great made financial contributions to the construction of the temple and this wonderful temple was completed before the end of the 4th century B.C. The commotion caused by the civil wars in Rome, the economic problems and the alluvial infilling of the bay strained the financial resources of the Temple of

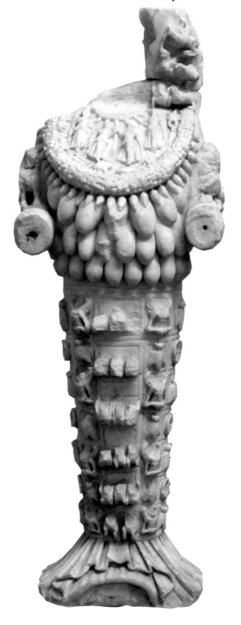

Artemis. The organized precautions, began under the Council in the 6 5th centuries B.C., came into effect during the reign of Emperor Augustus and all the borders, paths and drainage within the temenos wall, which was made of ashlar stone blocks covered in inscribed notices, were inspected and repaired. According to Strabo, the temenos wall was 1 stadion's distance from the temple and the temnos wall marked the border for those people seeking sanctuary under the protection of Artemis. Later during the reign of Emperor Titus (79-81 A.D.), large scale renovations were conducted in the sacred place. The Artemision was ravaged by the Goths in 263 A.D. but the real devastation came in 400 A.D. when the cult of Artemis ended and the altar, along with the surrounding colonnade and pediment were destroyed. The torn down temenos wall was reused during the Late Antique period in the construction of the Church of Mary and the erection of the Bishop's Palace. Much material from the Artemision was reused in the Basilica of St. John and in the construction of its outer walls. The Temple of Artemis was discovered for the British Museum in 1869 by the English railroad engineer J. T. Wood after a seven year search, during which he suffered badly from malaria. In these lengthy searches Wood found another classical platform upon an Archaic podium, in the traces of the foundation of the Late Classical temple and sent them to England, to the British Museum. His successor on behalf of the British Museum, the Englishman D. G. Hogarth recommenced excavations in 1904/05. Not only did he investigate the temple of Artemis, but also the older foundations within the court of the temple. New excavations, initiated by the Australian Museum of Archeology in 1965, continue today.

THE BATHS OF ISA BEY

There were four baths in the city of Ayasuluk, today called Seljuk, dating from the rule over the city by the Aydınoğulları Emirs and the Early Ottomans (1350-1450). The fact that baths were frequently constructed and were elaborate, exhibiting the characteristics of their periods indicate these bath were erected during the golden age of the city of Ayasuluk, when it was the capital of an important and wealthy Emirate-state, in part because Ayasuluk was a major trade centre, visited by many merchants from the Latin west in the 14th and 15th centuries and was also the focus of a rich agricultural hinterland. For sound seismic, as well as for decorative reasons in the constructions of these baths, courses of stone and courses of bricks were used in the walls and only bricks for the domes and vaults. The decorations in the baths extended to the domes and on the pedentives of the domes. Despite the similarities between these four baths, all of them had different plans. The relative position of the dressing-robing areas in these four baths is today unclear. In the period before the excavation of the Baths of Isa Bey, the warm section, the hot section, the higher walls of the furnace, with the domes and vaults covering these rooms, had been demolished. During the excavations the floor of the magnificent dressing area was unearthed; however the walls and the superstructure were not found.

From current information it is thought to have had a wooden roof and a cross-like and four cornered celled plan was employed in the construction of this bath house. With later additions, it was converted into a double bath. The stucco (a mixture of plaster and marble powder) decorations on the inside of the domes and roofs are exceedingly fine.

THE MOSQUE OF ISA BEY

When looking down from the Church of St. John, at the entrance to the plain, which has been infilled through alluvial deposition brought by the River Cayster over the centuries, there stands the Mosque of Isa Bey. It was constructed by order of Isa Bey of the Aydınoğulları Emirate in 1375. It has a tetragonal plan, close to a square, measuring 56.53 x 48.68 m. In the Mosque of Isa Bey the minarets were located in the west and east corners of the actual area of worship. Today only the western minaret made of bricks, remains in part, standing. Glazed bricks were used in the construction of the

pedestal and in the body of both of these minarets. Even though the eastern and northern facades of the mosque, constructed from ashlar masonry, are plain, the western front was covered with marble slabs. The portal, in the middle of the western facade, has some of the characteristics of earlier 13th

century Seljuk architecture. The monumental portal was made of white and yellowish stones and surrounded by a carved moulding and the window frames draw attention with their elaborate embellishments. The inscription (Kitabe), which was above the door and measuring 1 x 6 m. has been lost. There is a construction notice below the door arch and it states "the Mosque was constructed by an architect from Damascus named Ali on the order of Isa Bey of the Aydınoğulları Beylik in 776 (H)". On proceeding into the court from this highly decorated gate, one sees in the courtyard a polygonal water-tank with a

fountain, the court surrounded by porches on three sides. The columns and the column capitals used in the porches were reused material. It is known that the porches were covered by wooden roofs. The area where acts of worship were carried out in the mosque was reached by passing through the jagged arched three gates, supported by small columns. This area for prayer was divided into two sections by four great granite columns. The mihrap was covered by two domes, each with a diameter of 9 m. The interior of the domes was covered in blue and turquoise glazed tiles. The marble mirhap has been restored.

THE CHURCH OF ST. JOHN

According to the historian Eusebios, St. John returned to Ephesus with Mary after being banished from Jerusalem between 37 and 42 A.D. He continued to write the Bible after the execution of St. Paul and after a period he died here at Ephesus. Following his will, he was buried in the southern foothills of Ayasuluk Hill. First a wooden-roofed Early Christian Church was constructed in the 5th century over a simple graveyard and crypts were established within this church. In the middle of the 6th century, a monumental cross-in-plan basilica with domes was constructed by Emperor Justinianus (Justinian) replacing this earlier church. With the moving of the Ephesians to Ayasuluk, the Basilica of St. John took over the position of the earlier Bishop's Church at Ephesus. Ayasuluk Hill was encircled with walls constructed in the 7th century A.D. to protect the basilica and the related structures against Muslim raids. The material collected from the ruins of the Temple of Artemis, which had been largely demolished, were reused in the construction of these walls. The outer part of the walls was also constructed from material brought from other structures at Ephesus; its inner parts were filled with mortar and rubble stone and it was lined with towers to increase its strength. In the construction of these supporting towers, a pentagonal plan was generally employed; with a circular plan used in the west and a tetragonal plan in the south. The wall had a total of four gates and twenty towers. The strong, main entrance gate in the south was known as the "Gate of Pursuit". There were two square-in-plan towers on either side of this gate. There was an arched entrance in the middle of these two towers. On the arch there were a frieze with ivy, figures of Eros gathering grapes in the vineyard and a piece of a tomb which had a carved relief of grape vines. In the 19th century a second piece of this tomb, which depicted young girls narrating "the recognition of Achilles by Odysseus among the daughters of King Lykomedes on the Island of Skiros" and armed men, was taken to England and is today in the Museum at Woburn Abbey. Two phases of construction were observed in the walls surrounding and supporting the Basilica. The first of these phases was the construction of an additional terrace to the church during the reign of Justinianus, with stones and bricks employed in the construction of these walls. The second phase, comprised those walls constructed as a defence against Muslim raids in the 7-8th century A.D., with the inner parts of these walls filled with mortar and rubble stone. The Basilica, which is of a cross plan, is 130 m. long and was entered through the Narthex Gate. There were five gates from the narthex leading into the middle and side naves. It had a court (atrium) which was covered, with supporting columns in its middle. The middle and side naves were covered by 6 domes. These domes covered the burial grounds with the middle dome larger and higher than the others.

THE CHURCH OF ST. JOHN

The columns separating the naves were monoliths of blue marble. On the Byzantine Ionic capitals were carved the monograms of Emperor Justinianus and his wife Theodora. These monograms provide proof that the Emperor contributed to the construction of this church. There was a large ambon in front of the dais in the middle nave. The dais or the burial grounds were two steps higher than the floor of the church. It is known that one of them belonged to St. John. There was a crypt under the dais. There were three tombs in the crypt, one of which is understood to have belonged to St. John. The chapel, having been constructed outside the northern transept and planned together with the Office of Revenues, was actually turned into a chapel in the 10-11th century and the depictions in the apse, of St. John on the right; Jesus Christ in the middle and an unknown Saint on the left, are in a very well preserved condition. The Office of Revenues, situated to the left of the chapel, was a two-storey structure with a centralized plan. There were cross-in-plan parts and corner rooms surrounding the circular area in the middle. The sacred relics and treasures of the church were stored within these rooms. Furthermore a Baptistry was constructed in the 5th century A.D. with the basilica, with the remains of the wooden roof belonging to the period prior to the reign of Justinianus still to be seen today as, when the new church was constructed, it was preserved and its function continued. The apsed chamber to the east was the sacred chamber in which prayers after baptisms were performed. The central area of the Baptistry is reached from the western door of this octagonal-in-plan structure. There was a circular pool for baptism in the middle of the floor, with the sides of this pool consisting of stairs of three-steps. The adjacent square pool was where the sacred water was kept. The apsed chamber to the far west, a symmetrical copy of that in the east, was used for the same purpose.

THE MUSEUM OF EPHESUS

With the establishment of the Republic of Turkey, the necessary importance was given to ancient remains and to museum studies; museums with extensive cultural responsibilities were established and storage museums were also established. The archeological richness of Seljuk and its vicinity and the archeological excavations that had continued from 1863 required a storage-museum to be constructed here in 1929. Over time, because of the increasing number of finds from Ephesus and its vicinity, this building proved insufficient and a modern museum was opened in 1964. In later years the main building was extended and in 1976 the museum reached its present size. The redecoration and exhibition works in the museum halls in 1994 continue from time to time with the arrival of new finds, with most of the artifacts exhibited in the museum coming from the excavations at Ephesus. In addition to these, there are also artifacts from the Temple of Artemis, the Monumental Tomb of St. John, from the Cave of the Seven Sleepers and other excavations and from the rescue excavations conducted by the Museum in the area. In the First Hall are exhibited finds from the residences of the rich people of Roman Ephesus. In the Second Hall are the monumental water-supply fountains that decorated the streets of the city and the associated sculptures. The court is reached from the small

chamber where the coin finds and terracotta figurines are exhibited. There are architectural artifacts in the garden and displays related to the local handicrafts, which are rapidly disappearing, around the garden and there are the Museums of the Ottoman Bazaar and Baths. From this court there is entrance to the chamber in which the finds from tombs are exhibited; and from there, there is an entrance to the chamber where the finds from the Temple of Artemis and the statues of Artemis of Ephesus are exhibited, forming an important part of this museum. The visit around the museum ends with the display of the finds relating to the Roman cult of the Emperors and the Portrait Hall.

THE HALL OF FINDS FROM THE SLOPE HOUSES

Here the furniture, statues (Hygieia, Zeus), friezes and small finds from Slope Houses No. 1 and 2 are exhibited. On the left of the entrance there is a table and an altar dedicated to Zeus. From the left; In the first display case: the earthenware Asklepios capital, a small altar with snakes, equipment used in medicine and cosmetics, items unearthed from graves, scales and other units of measure, jewellery in various glass containers and adornments are exhibited. In the second display case: relief cast earthenware plates, small capitals and ivory statuettes, bronze statuettes of gods and goddesses, with, in the middle a glass tray, two small busts; and on

the right, toys, flutes, discs, medical instruments and figures made of bone are exhibited. There is a reconstruction of a section of the "Socrates Room" (original and impressionistic) from the Slope House, friezes on the wall belonging to various eras, the statuettes of the hunter Goddess Artemis and of Socrates in the niche and the Muse Clio on the left. There is the bronze statuette of the Egyptian priest of Amun in the small display case on the left of the exit. There is a bust of Tiberius wearing armor, a bronze snake and a portrait bust of Livia, the bust of the poet Menandros, the portrait of a priest and a priestess, an earthenware statuette of a pigmy in the embedded display, a marble statue of Priapos, a bust of the Emperor Marcus Aurelius wearing armor and an honorary pedestal of an athlete with a triumphal garland. In the displays in the middle of the hall: there is an archaic marble statue of Artemis, a bronze bust of a philosopher, the river god lying on a bed supported by two

dolphins, the protom of a bronze boxer, a foldable table and chair, a marble sink on the floor, an ivory frieze and plates depicting the war are displayed.

THE HALL OF FOUNTAIN FINDS:

In this hall there are the monumental fountains that provided water to the city and decorated the streets and the

statues from three of the monumental fountain structures of Ephesus are exhibited here. On the left of the entrance there are the bust of Zeus and the torso of Aphrodite. In the middle there is the statue of a resting warrior from the Fountain of Pollio, one of the most important fountains of Ephesus. In the section to the right; there are the three tritons decorating the Fountain of C. Laekanius Bassus (Hydekdokheion) and the torso of a Satyr, two statues of Nemesis, a statue of Aphrodite, a torso, statues of two women and the honorary pedestal of the benefactor. Three marble game pieces are displayed in the middle of this section. On the east wall between the honorary pedestal and the exit there is the bust of the commander, the bust of Hermes, Lysimmakhos, two male busts, two busts of Artemis, two women portraits and one column capital. In the section to the left; there is the mythological Polyphemos Group, which decorated the niche of the

Fountain of Pollio. There is the statue of Polyphemos on the middle rock and Odysseos, who is trying to intoxicate him by offering him wine. On the right there is a friend of Polyphemos, who is sharpening the wooden stake to blind Polyphemos, and on the left there are two friends who are bringing wine to Odysseos in an animal skin. In front of Polyphemos lie two Greeks, he has killed to eat them.

The Polyphemos Group was reused in this fountain. There are more columns carved in the shape of vines with human figures, exhibited together with the statue of a naked Dionysus, a reclining Satyr, the statues of a man and woman dressed and carrying a wand, a dressed Dionysus, Androklos and his dog on the supporting pediment and the statue of Aphrodite, all of which are statues that decorated the front of the Fountain of Traianus at the side of Kuretes Street.

THE CHAMBER OF SMALL FINDS AND EROS

In the display to the left of the entrance to this chamber are the marble statues of Eros, a block from a frieze of Eros, a masked Eros, Oinochoe and an Eros with rabbits. There are figurines with Eros and oil lamps on the wall display. There are statues of Eros with dolphins and a part of a tomb with dolphins in the small displays.

There is the carved relief statue of Eros in the niche and there are earthenware figurines of Eros in the displays. Most of this section is connected to Eros and related artifacts. In the large display are the coins from Early Ephesus and the finds of treasures, an ivory plate of Eros and a bronze statue of Eros with dolphins. This section ends .

THE CHAMBER OF TOMB FINDS

On the left of the entrance In the first display: These finds from Ephesus are historically very important. The earthenware artifacts displayed in this room are Mycenean Era vessels dating from 1400-1375 B.C. Many artifacts, such as the double handled vase with octopus ornaments and krater, rhyton and amphoriskos were found in the excavation of a tomb near the Persecution Gate of the Church of St. John. In the second display contains: The weapons and other finds from the excavation of a tomb in Didyma dating from the Early Bronze Age. In the third display: Are the earthenware figurines from the vicinity of the city of Metropolis, the statue of Harpokrates, who closed his mouth with his finger, from the Late Antique tomb in the Governmental Agora of Ephesus, the statue of a ram and askos, lekythos, kantharos, unguanteirum, oil lamp, megare and other bowls. On the right of the entrance: A tomb obelisk depicting a wake around the Church of Mary and on the right an extraordinarily detailed relief of a wake from Slope House No. 2 are displayed. There are four ostotheks, two of which have lids, from around Ephesus and an inscribed block behind the partition wall. By the exit door there are tomb obelisks depicting a farewell scene and next to it there is the single-figure tomb obelisk of Olympias and other tomb obelisks.

In the display of Glass Finds: As well as various bracelets, unguantariums and other bottles, there are sand moulded amphoriskos and alabastron, which were recovered from the tomb underneath the Government Agora. There are the Cybele Reliefs to the left of the exit door. Cybele is generally depicted with her lions. Ephesus is the source of the culture of Artemis. In this area are offering reliefs and statuettes concerning the Mother goddess Cybele brought from various places. Another depiction of Cybele has a young god (Hermes) and an old god (Zeus) on either side of her.

THE LARGE COURT

There are tombstones, reliefs, column capitals and architectural elements in the museum's court with a pool. There are two sundials in the middle of the court, ostotheks, tombs and tomb obelisks on the right side of the wall. Against the entrance there are the statues of two marble dolphins and Eros by the pool and there are various column capitals from Ephesus, dating from different periods, from the Archaic to Byzantium and Seljuk beneath the reconstruction of the pediment of the Polyphemos group at the back. There is entrance to the ethnography museum by a bridge over the mosaics from a Roman villa. On the right side of the entrance to the court there are the depictions of prophet Abraham sacrificing his son and two meander frieze blocks from the Altar of the Artemision. There are the columns from the Monument of the Belevi Tomb on the right of the sundial in the middle of the court, a portion of the roof decorations on the left and a highly decorated marble tomb.

THE CHAMBER OF ARTEMIS EPHESIA

In this chamber, the finds from the Artemision and associated with the cult of Artemis are exhibited as well asfigures of Artemis Ephesia.

THE STATUES OF ARTEMIS

The elegant and colossal marble statue of Ephesus Artemis exhibited in the large niche on the left dates from the 1st century A.D. There is a garment over her head, attached with a circlet and she has a three layered crown decorated with gryphons and sphinxes. It is possible to see this crown in the Temple of Artemis. She has a pendant around her neck. The symbols of fertility and source of life, which are shown in the shape of eggs, cover her whole breast. Each section is filled with animal reliefs symbolizing the power of the Goddess. Furthermore, the bee ornaments, which are the symbol of the city of Ephesus, are depicted. Only the tips of her toes are seen from under her skirt. Opposite there is the elegant and magnificent marble Ephesus Artemis brought from the Prytaneion in Ephesus.

The statue was unearthed during excavations around Ephesus City Hall in 1956. This Ephesus Artemis is the most beautiful and precious in the museum and dates from 125-175 A.D. It differs from the other depictions of Artemis with the necklace adorned with the symbols of the Zodiac (stars and astrology). Her toes are seen from under her skirt. There are two of her deer at her sides. It is a copy of the wooden statue that was in the Temple of Artemis. On its right, there is a statue of Artemis which is smaller than the average human being and doesn't have a head. There are the palm frieze blocks from the altar, a part of a lead water pipe, an altar with reliefs of Moses, the torso and bust of a horse belonging to the roof decoration and a marble bust that is thought to have fallen from a carved column. On the left of the exit door there are arranged the cornice pieces and a lion headed capital (gargoyle) belonging to an upturned edge of the roof. To the right of the entrance door there are double carved relief orthostat, meander

figured blocks and an amazon carved relief moulage (the original is in the Museum of Ephesus in Vienna) collected from the altar pedestals. There are also the artifacts found in the excavations of the Artemision; goddess figurines made of gold, ivory, bone, amber, bronze and earthenware, statuettes of women, fibulas, busts of lions and bulls, peacocks, gryphon protoms and animal figurines, pendants, askos, aryballos and oil lamps.

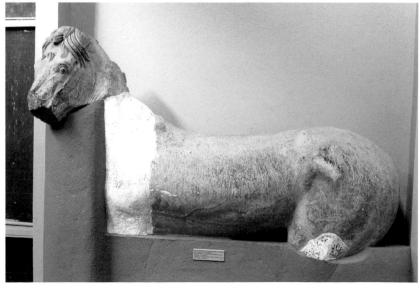

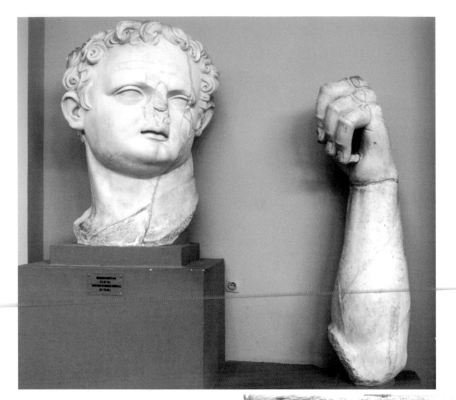

THE CHAMBER OF THE IMPERIAL CULT

This is the last hall of the museum. On the left of the entrance there is a frieze of four blocks brought from the porch of the Temple of Hadrianus. Its reliefs depict Androklos and the legend of the establishment of Ephesus. On the first block the legend concerning the mounted Androklos killing the wild boar is depicted; on the second block the legend of the sacrificial rites of Greeks in front of an altar and the escape of the Amazons are depicted; on the third block the cortege of Dionysus and on the fourth block scenes from the assembly of gods are depicted. After the friezes, the marble busts of two men, Augustus with a garland of oak leaves on his head, the busts of Empress Livia and Traianus, the statue of Commodus

behind the screen, a priest of the Imperial Cult, Emperor Balbinus and the bust of Julia Paula are exhibited.The altar, which carries the depictions showing the sacrifice of a bull, various weapons and warriors from the Temple of Domitianus is also in this chamber. Not only the Parth reliefs found in later excavations, but also the moulage (most of which is in the

Museum of Ephesus in Vienna) that forms part of a block are also exhibited in this chamber
To the right of the entrance is the statue of the Proconsul Stephanos, marble pieces (head, left arm) of the giant, acrolid statue of Titus and the large statues of Emperor Augustus and his wife Livia, monuments that are certainly worth seeing.

THE HOUSE OF THE VIRGIN MARY

The persecution of the Christians by the Romans and the conservative Jews increased after the Roman Emperor Caligula (37-41 A.D.) during his visit to Jerusalem ordered that his statue be put in the synagogues. Even the Apostles could no longer remain in Jerusalem and they decided to scatter to various lands in order to save their lives and spread the Bible. While sharing in the Apostolic duties, Roman Asia Minor was given to St. John. The Apostle John, taking with him the Virgin Mary who had been entrusted to his care by Jesus, arrived near Ephesus in the Roman state of Asia Minor between 37 and 42 A.D. The Apostle John and Mary were as uncomfortable in Ephesus as they had been in Jerusalem and they lived for a period in the Church of Mary.

This story was confirmed by the Council of Ephesus held in 431 A.D. It is obvious John and Mary were not happy in Ephesus because during that period an idol-worshipping pagan Roman emperor was in power. Consequently they chose to live in a mose secluded area on the western front of Aladağ, 7 km. to the south of Ephesus, 420 m. above sea level, on Solmisos-Aladağ, which was a place suitable for protection and shelter and where they had a house constructed for themselves. It is assumed that the Virgin Mary lived the rest of her life and died in this house in her 60s in 45 A.D. and that the Apostle John secretly buried her. With the passage of time this house became derilict and its whereabouts was forgotten. St. John thought that a new goddess or an idol could be created to represent the Virgin Mary, since the people of Ephesus were in the habit of worshipping

goddesses, as with the cult of Artemis-Diana. John took a precaution of confidentiality concerning this matter which was called "the Law of Confidentiality". In the years following Marys' death the tyrannical persecution by the Roman idol-worshippers of the Christians continued. It is thought that the Apostle John took these precautions to prevent any damage by the pagans to the tomb of the Mother of Jesus. Gregory of Tours (538-594) was the first author to mention the small church in a mountain near Ephesus in his work, a combination of history and legend. The German nun, Katerin Emmerik (between 1774- 1824), who had been paralyzed all her life, spiritually connected with the Virgin Mary by going into trances and she collected the information she obtained in this manner in a book called "The Life of the Virgin Mary". In 1881 a Priest named Gouyet from the Paris episcopacy decided to go to Ephesus in order to determine if the house that is described in this book entitled "The Life of Virgin Mary" as belonging to Mary was correct in its description or not. The Archbishop of Izmir (Smyrna), Monseigneur Timoni encouraged him in his research in this matter. According to his research, Gouyet claimed that he had found the House of Virgin Mary (a small church, constructed upon an antique structure, dating from the 13th century during the Byzantine period) and reported this news to the Paris episcopacy, to Monseigneur Timoni

and to Rome. However his report was not believed. Ten years later the Lazarite M. Jung, one of the nuns of the French Hospital at Izmir, and the Lazarite Priest Eugene Poulin, the principal of the French College of Izmir, a Hebrew expert and a person who knew the Jewish traditions very well, decided to organize a trip to Ephesus. Two priests and two Catholics were assigned to this research. The team of four people started out on the 27th of July, 1891. On the 29th of July 1891 around 11 o'clock, they arrived in a very exhausted condition at a plain planted with tobacco. As they were

thirsty, they requested water from the women working in the farm, but they replied, "We ran out of water, but you will find water if you go to the monastery". They pointed to a seriously damaged structure. After they drank the water, the four researchers looked around and they were dazzled. The destroyed house, the mountain behind the house and the sea in front of them, all of the details provided by Katerin Emmerik concerning the appearance and location of the House of Mary were accurate. They examined the lines describing the house in the book "The Life of Virgin Mary". In the book it said that both Ephesus and the sea were visible from the hillside where the House of Mary was situated. For two days they investigated the hills and apart from the place where this devastated structure stood, both Ephesus and the sea could not be seen from anywhere else and so they knew they had found the House of Mary. On December the first, 1892 a committee of 12 people, consisting of seven priests and five laymen, under the presidency of Monseigneur Timoni, went to the House of Mary. The committee realized that the similarities between the House and the descriptions provided by Katerin

Emmerik were obvious; there and then an official written report was quickly issued and was signed by the members of the committee. The nun Marie de Mandat Grancey then purchased this place and paid for the repairs made to the House and for various works in its vicinity which were completed by 1894. Firstly a channel was opened to the water supply, practical paths providing access were made, terraces were constructed below the small church and a vegetable garden was made. Later, a house was constructed as a shelter for the nuns and the visitors. The largest problem was with the small church and in order to protect and preserve the current structure, a glass roof was erected over these four walls. In 1895 Pope Leon XIII, the Director of The French Papacy Seminar and the chairman of the committee, who was working on ceremonial methods in the Near East and T. R. R. Eschbach in Jerusalem, who had heard of the discovery of the House of Mary, requested from Mr Poulin a companion to go to the House. Mr Jung was appointed as the companion. On his return to Rome, T. R. R. Eschbach reported to Pope Leon XIII and showed him the photographs that had been taken. After examining them, the Pope kept them and issued a bulletin called "Panaya Kapulu", presented as the responsibility of Monseigneur Timoni. In 1931 on the anniversary of the Council of Ephesus, Monseigneur Roncalli, Archbishop of Bulgaria (later Pope John XXIII), and Monseigneur Tonna, the Archbishop of Izmir, went to the church at Ephesus in which the Council was held; however, owing to the state of the road they were unable to reach the House of the Virgin Mary. Raymond Pere, who made the friezes-frescoes? still today in the Church of St. Policarp in Izmir

researches will generate results of great importance. According to the beliefs of the Lazarites in Izmir, this church, also called the "Monastery with Three Gates", was erected over the place where Mary spent her last years. These local statements dating from the 19th century have not yet been confirmed through archeological research. In the meantime the ownership of this place was transferred from various people to Mr Euzet, and it was then gifted to the Association of "Panaya Kapulu" in 1951. This association was recognized

(Smyrna), constructed a small altar of marble in this small church. In this period olive trees were planted on both sides of the path leading to the small church housing the statue of the Virgin Mary. The Turkish Government constructed a road in 1950 providing access for vehicles to the church, which previously could only be reached along difficult paths and the cross-vaulted small church, which is described as the "House of Mary", is reached at the end of this road. This church was constructed on top of the foundations of a Byzantine structure thought to date from the 13th century. Today, the upper limit of the remains of these earlier foundations, are indicated by a red band. The structure was entered through a gate with niches on both sides. Passing through the arched entrance area,

the apsed section was reached and there was a bedroom on the southern side. The first remains to be found were a ruined wall and a cistern 100 m. from the house and in the excavations conducted by Professor Prandi in 1966, two tiled tombs containing two skeletons were found and the heads of these skeletons faced the House of the Virgin Mary. In these excavations two coins dating from the reigns of Emperors Constantinos and Justinianus were found. These finds indicated the building had remained in use during the reign of Justinianus in the mid 6th century. These excavations were then terminated because of the lack of discoveries and finds from the area but it is hoped that new archeological excavations will be conducted in this area and it is hoped these new

by the Turkish Government and was later renamed, "the Pope John XXIII), and Monseigneur Tonna, the Archbishop of Izmir, went to the church at Ephesus in which the Council was held; however, owing to the state of the road they were unable to reach the House of the Virgin Mary. Raymond Pere, who made the friezes-frescoes? still today in the Church of St. Policarp in Izmir (Smyrna), constructed a small

altar of marble in this small church. In this period olive trees were planted on both sides of the path leading to the small church housing the statue of the Virgin Mary. The Turkish Government constructed a road in 1950 providing access for vehicles to the church, which previously could only be reached along difficult paths and the cross-vaulted small church, which is described as the "House of Mary", is reached at the end of this road. This church was constructed on top of the foundations of a Byzantine structure thought to date from the 13th century. Today, the upper limit of the remains of these earlier foundations, are indicated by a red band. The structure was entered through a gate with niches on both sides. Passing through the arched entrance area, the apsed section was reached and there was a bedroom on the southern side. The first remains to be found were a ruined wall and a cistern 100 m. from the house and in the excavations conducted by Professor Prandi in 1966, two tiled tombs containing two skeletons were found and the heads of these skeletons faced the House of the Virgin Mary. In these excavations two coins dating from the reigns of Emperors Constantinos and Justinianus were found. These finds indicated the building had remained in

use during the reign of Justinianus in the mid 6th century. These excavations were then terminated because of the lack of discoveries and finds from the area but it is hoped that new archeological excavations will be conducted in this area and it is hoped these new archeological researches will generate results of great importance. According to the beliefs of the Lazarites in Izmir, this church, also called the "Monastery with Three Gates", was erected over the place where Mary spent her last years. These local statements dating from the 19th century have not yet been confirmed through archeological research. In the meantime the ownership of this place was

transferred from various people to Mr Euzet, and it was then gifted to the Association of "Panaya Kapulu" in 1951. This association was recognized by the Turkish Government and was later renamed, "the Association of the House of Virgin Mary". This association was authorized to collect the funds necessary for the restoration and for the better care of this ancient Christian sanctuary. Five years after the discovery of the House, in 1896, the first religious visit to the House of Mary was conducted. According to the statement of Mr Euzet, two trains carried around 1300 to 1400 pilgrims from Izmir to Ephesus. In 1906 the first guests for religious purposes arrived from abroad led by Professor

Miner and Kayser the Priest. Between 1914 and 1927 there were no religious ceremonies held in this place. In 1932 the Lazarite priests, who wanted to continue the traditions and customs of the period prior to the outbreak of the First World War and the nuns of the French Hospital organized a visit to the House of the Virgin Mary with their students. This practice continued for four years. But no visits were made between 1937 and 1949. In 1949 a ceremony was held in this small hypaethral church for a group from Istanbul which came to visit the House, under the presidency of Archbishop Descuffi. In 1950 Monseigneur Gschwind of Basel, who had studied the antiquities of Asia Minor in Istanbul during the Second World War, organized a pilgrimage to Ephesus from Istanbul on the 1st day of November to celebrate the belief in the Assumption of the Virgin. When Pope Paul VI came to Turkey in 1967, he went from Istanbul to Ephesus on the 26th of July to worship the Virgin Mary and during his visit to the House, he prayed in front of the altar for a long time. After lighting the oil lamp embellished with the heraldic devices of the Roman Catholic religion, he left the House of the Virgin Mary. His successor Pope John Paul II came

to Turkey in November 30th 1979 and visiting the House of the Virgin Mary with the assembled pilgrims and tourists, he conducted a ceremony there and then left. Most recently on November 29th 2006, Pope Benedictus XVI visited the House of the Virgin Mary. The statue of Mary in the apse of the church was placed there a century ago. Next to the apse are the other parts of the House, such as the kitchen and the bedroom. The House of Mary, which is believed to have healing properties, the water flowing from the fountains in this place is believed to heal the diseased, is visited by Muslims as well as Christians and offerings are made here. There is a pool of water 100 m. north of the House. Every year on the 15th of August, commemorative ceremonies for the Virgin Mary are held at the House of the Virgin Mary.

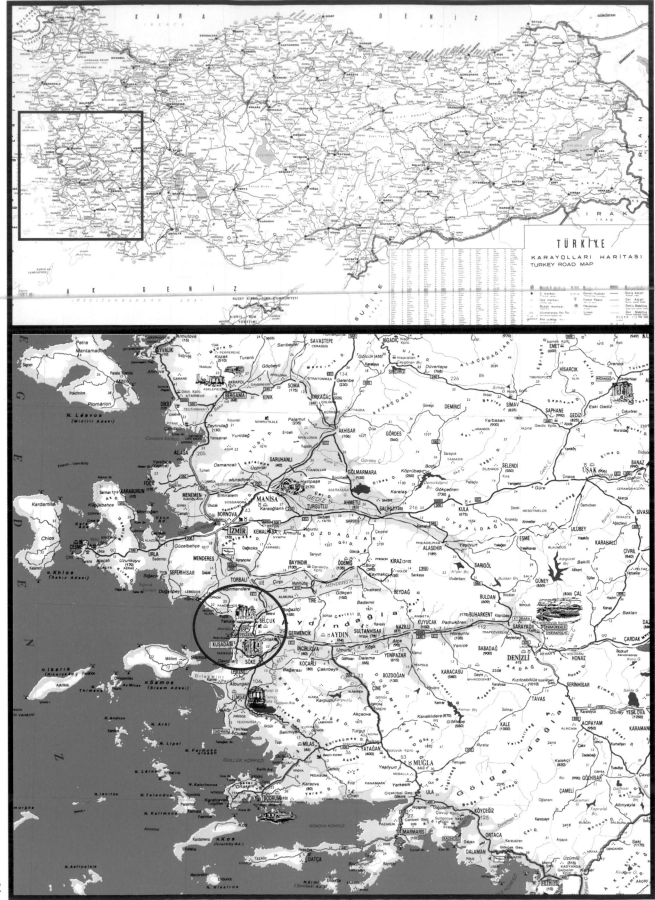